1

Bow Ties of Bravery Alphabet Series

Brought to you by Lise Steeves
of
Lises' Library

Bow Ties of Bravery Alphabet Series

Dedication

The Bow Ties of Bravery series is dedicated for those of you looking for something a little different.

This Book Belongs To:

_____

Clark
The Camel

Liked to climb

Written & Illustrated
By: Lise Steeves

Clark liked living in the Desert.

There is warm sand, cool water holes and tall mountains.

Growing up, he saw all the greatest Camels climb the craziest heights.

Clark dreamed of climbing the biggest mountain of all, "The Knee Chatter".

The next day Clark decided, "What better time than now to give climbing a chance."

Clark went to share the great news with his friend Clarence.

"Hello Clarence!" Clark was awfully chipper.

"Good morning Clark, why are you so happy today?" Clarence asked.

"I'm going to climb THE KNEE CHATTER!" Clark announced.

"That's great Clark, but you have never climbed before. Maybe you should start with something a little smaller", advised Clarence.

Clark and Clarence went to a mini mountain called Confidence Cliff.

"Okay" said Clarence; "let's see what you can do!"

Clark charged at Confidence Cliff.

No sooner was Clark half way up than he came CRASHING down.

Clark was HURT!

"Can you move?" asked Clarence.

"Yes, but it's my ankle", said Clark.

"We better get you to the clinic",
Clarence said.

Clark was sad he was hurt.

Confidence Cliff had crushed Clarks
"Can do" attitude.

"Don't be so sad Clark", Clarence said.

"But I'm hurt", cried Clark.

"Clark, you made a choice and were committed to it. That shows great confidence, which you should be proud of", Clarence said.

"Now you can contemplate your climb of Confidence Cliff", Clarence said.

"What do you mean, Contemplate?" asked Clark.

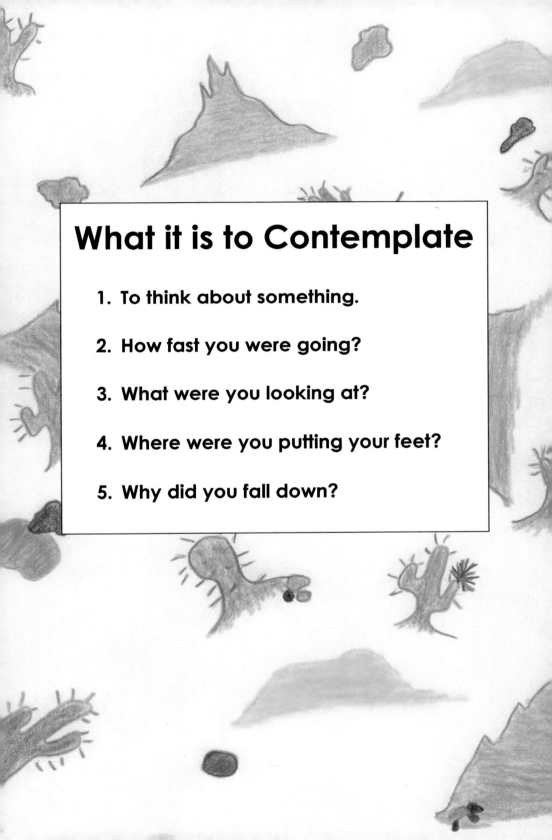

What it is to Contemplate

1. To think about something.

2. How fast you were going?

3. What were you looking at?

4. Where were you putting your feet?

5. Why did you fall down?

Clark was feeling better, and was back walking, running, and jumping like his old self.

He had contemplated his climb of Confidence Cliff.

Clark thought of things he should do to become a great climber.

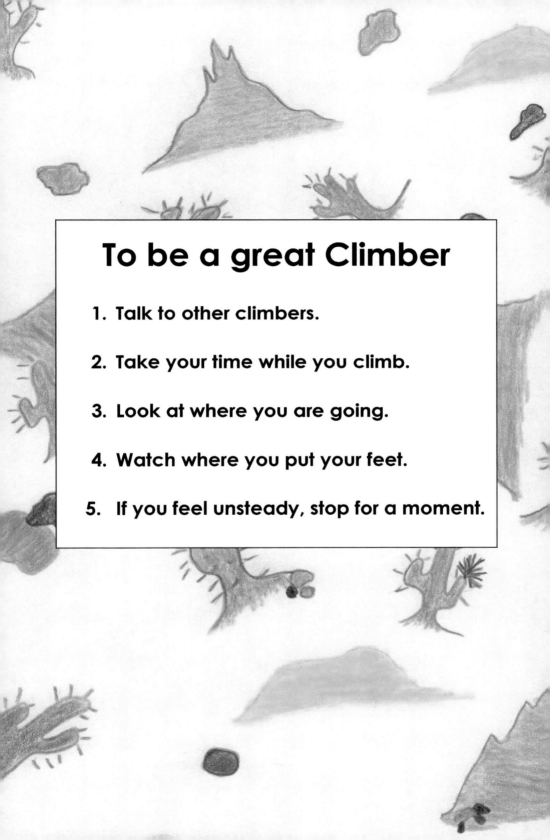

To be a great Climber

1. Talk to other climbers.

2. Take your time while you climb.

3. Look at where you are going.

4. Watch where you put your feet.

5. If you feel unsteady, stop for a moment.

"Maybe if I climb different things, that will improve my climbing skills", said Clark

Clarence saw Clark eyeing up a BIG POKEY CACTUS.

"The possibilities are endless", said Clarence.

"Totally!" Clark said with a grin.

The next day Clarence was walking by the BIG POKEY CACTUS and saw Clark standing atop.

"CLARK!" hollered Clarence, "how in the world did you get up there?"

Clark explained, "I used the big pokies that stick out, like steps."

"But didn't you get poked by some of them?" questioned Clarence.

"When I first tried I did, but then I got a stick and cracked off the ones that I knew would get me", Clark laughed.

Clark started to run, "Come on Clarence;
let's go back to Confidence Cliff."

"Clark! Wait for me!" Clarence yelled.

He started laughing, happy his friend was full of confidence once again.

Clark climbed with self-control all the way to the top of Confidence Cliff.

After looking at the wondrous view, Clark climbed down, contemplating each move so he would not crash again.

On his way down, Clark told Clarence, "It's time to train for The Knee Chatter Mountain. I believe I can do it!"

Question & Answer

1. What was Clark's goal?

2. At first did Clark think about what he needed to do?

3. Did Clark get hurt?

4. Did Clark use self-control when he climbed down?

5. What happened to Clark's confidence?

Question & Answer

6. Did Clark contemplate what he needed to do after he got hurt?

7. Was Clarence supportive of Clark?

8. Could Clark's confidence be crushed?

9. Did Clark learn to control himself?

10. Will Clark continue to try?

Lise Steeves is a published writer. Miss Steeves' first publication came out in the late 1980's with her letter "To the Unknown Soldier" through St. Benedict Catholic School. Writing has always been a dream of hers and she is happy to bring it to you now under "Lises' Library", the "Bow Ties of Bravery Alphabet Series."

The Bow Tie of Bravery is there for all of us in good times and bad. Whether it is visible or imaginary it is there to help give us grace, strength and courage as we face life while we grow.

First in the

Bow Ties of Bravery Alphabet Series

By Lises' Library

Next in line for the

Bow Ties of Bravery Alphabet Series

By Lises' Library

Dave
The Donkey

Ella
The Emu